"You can't be in a hurry to read this latest addition to Helena's *Purposeful Mind* series. Each poem is a meditation within itself, deserving the contemplation the author suggests in the writing. I highly recommend you gift yourself with some internal exploration and be guided by her words that are so simply put, yet cannot be ignored."

— *Christine Gabb, Emotional Transformation Coach*

"When I'm in my head too much, worrying about this and that, all I have to do is read from this beautiful book to feel soothed and peaceful again. These words so eloquently express how to be and will be of great benefit to anyone who seeks the truth. Thank you Helena for sharing this with the world!"

— *Sandy Calverley, Medical Transcriptionist*

"From the first poem in Helena Kalivoda's book, *Contemplation*, I was drawn deep within myself. Her words speak so gently and deeply. The flow of words and thoughts opened doors to many hallways within my consciousness that needed some light. The heartfelt connection that flows through Helena's words touches the deep stillness within. I suggest that you allow yourself a chance to expand your connection within, which is so beautifully expressed in this book."

— *Sharon Carne, author, speaker, musician, recording artist, founder of Sound Wellness*

CONTEMPLATION

Understanding Your Inner World

Purposeful Mind Series – Book Three

Other Books by Helena Kalivoda

AWAKEN!
Your Soul Is Calling

WAKE UP!
Your Heart Is Calling

WAKE UP!
Prosperity Is Calling

Purposeful Mind Series:

CREATION
Accessing Your Untapped Potential

ILLUMINATION
Getting to Know the Invisible You

CONTEMPLATION
Understanding Your Inner World

EVOLUTION
It Is Time for the New You

METAMORPHOSIS
What Else Is Possible?

CONTEMPLATION

Understanding Your Inner World

Purposeful Mind Series – Book Three

HELENA KALIVODA

AUDRENAR BOOKS

CONTEMPLATION
Understanding Your Inner World
Purposeful Mind Series – Book Three

Copyright ©2014 by Helena Kalivoda
Published by Audrenar Books

Library and Archives Canada Cataloguing in Publication

Kalivoda, Helena,
Contemplation / Helena Kalivoda.

Poems.
ISBN 978-0-9877521-2-3

I. Title.

PS8621.A469C66 2012 C811'.6 C2012-902412-0

The author designed the information to represent her opinion about the subject disclosed. The author obtained the information contained through personal experience and speaks from her perspective and experience. The author disclaims any liability, loss or risk incurred by individuals who act on the information contained herein.

Editing: Agnes L. Kirby
Cover art: original oil painting by Jaroslav Kalivoda

For more information on this book and other books by Helena Kalivoda visit www.booksbyhelena.ca.

*I am dedicating this series to my family
and to all who are searching to reconnect
with that part of Divinity we call Self.*

TABLE OF CONTENTS

ACKNOWLEDGEMENT 13

PREFACE 15

HONESTY

Honesty Brings You the Furthest....................................19

Emphasize Your Good Points 21

Dealing with Yourself..23

FEAR vs. JOY

Fear Is a Way of Postponing 27

Precarious Living 28

Don't Gravitate Toward Heavy.......................................29

Alleviate Your Worries...30

Brooding Is a Way to Misery 31

Activate Joy to Breed Joy 32

You Are a Free Bird...33

Make Your Life Fun..34

YOU ARE FIRST

You Are Worth Every Penny 39

Listen to Your Own Beat...40

Follow the Path of Your Desire 42

Don't Obey Your Ego 43

JUST BE

Being 47

Be like Nature, Just Be.......................................48

Nature Is the Way to Be.....................................49

Learn from Nature..50

Smell the Roses All the Time..............................52

Be Your Own 53

LOVE

Smell the Roses of Godly Love 57

Replace the Military with Love............................58

Bestow Your Love on All 60

Your Love Breeds Love.......................................62

Love 64

Earthly Love...65

Heavenly Love 67

Love as an Emotion of Your Life 69

Love Is Not Based on Duties 70

Through Love..72

Project Love at All Times 73

Love Is Knowing..74

Love Is a Melting Pot...75

Substance of the Universe...................................76

Love Is Life..77

God's Love Is an Endless Rapture 79

Your Heart Is the Seat of the Spirit.....................81

HEART

Your Heart Is Not Only a Pump.....................85
Keep Your Heart Clear...................................87
With All My Heart 88
I Love You 89
In Your Heart You Know It All 90
You Know That You Know............................92

SEXUALITY

Sex Is Pure if You Are Pure..........................95
Sex Is Not Keeping You Down......................96
Sexuality Is God's Gift 98

DREAMLAND

Contemplate on Your Dreams......................101
In Sleep You Contact God 102
But What Is a Dream?..................................103
Dreams Are Important 104

ABOUT THE AUTHOR...............................105

ACKNOWLEDGEMENT

Thank you, Spirit, for transmitting this inspiring material to me. Deep thanks to Agnes L. Kirby for offering her generous help in editing the *Purposeful Mind* series of five books.

I am appreciative of my family's support and of all my incarnate and spiritual muses for their presence in my life.

Helena Kalivoda

PREFACE

Contemplation, the third of five books in the *Purposeful Mind* series, deals with bringing conscious being-ness into doing-ness. The level of consciousness we bring to our daily lives is mirrored to us by the quality of our life experiences. Aspiring to change a condition in our external world without attending to our internal environment cannot bring the results we seek.

The main topics of this book include discourses on honesty, joy vs. fear, treating ourselves well, love, heart, sexuality and more.

Our present times are about remembering who we are. May this series help you to quicken the process of remembering your origins, and propel you on your path of awakening, as you evolve with grace and ultimately connect with your grand Self.

Helena Kalivoda

HONESTY

HONESTY BRINGS YOU THE FURTHEST

Honesty brings you the furthest.
Honesty about yourself,
honesty about others,
honesty toward yourself,
honesty about your brothers.
Honesty about your unending pleasures,
unending wretched small lost battles.
Honesty about yourself to yourself.

Honesty is the discourse we are having today.

Honesty is a treasured way of treating yourself
to receive the gifts of the Universe.
It is a way to connect with yourself,
as then the filmy veil of deceit,
even if very discreet, is not in the way.

Be honest with yourself, be a winner.
Be on the lookout of all
that is even slightly skewed,
that feels only slightly wrong.

Honesty opens the door to your success.
Honesty opens the door to your accreditation,
as an honest being touches both worlds,
world of humanity and Spirit.

Honesty is a treasured thing.
It is not difficult to see if you are honest
if you honestly look at your honesty.
Sounds like a recursion? Does it?

Well, it may seem like it,
but it is so simple
that I think you will like it.

Be honest with yourself.
Be honest with you
and all else falls into place,
and the virtue that you possess
will be returned to you.

Abracadabra it ain't.
Honesty is a treasured thing
that returns as a gift,
when you will be rewarded for your honesty
by honesty from others.

Do to yourself what you want others to do to you.
Do to yourself what feels right
and is not in any way
impeding others from enjoying their way.

Be yourself and enjoy being honest.
Honesty is a thing to cherish.

EMPHASIZE YOUR GOOD POINTS

Honesty to yourself, honesty in accepting
that you are naive when you are
or that you need a hand in certain areas.

Honest enough to admit that you need help
and to comprehend that you do not
embarrass yourself that way.

What is it you want to admit?

I am disorganized?
I am talkative?
I am not too focused?
I am not who I think I am?

Now, that's enough!
What you really need to do is
emphasize your good points
and build on those.

I am compassionate.
I am understanding.
I am helpful.
I am joyful.

Emphasize your good points
and you will be able to join
the ranks of those
whose satisfaction is not derived
from the praise of others

but is ingrained in them,
as they are kind to themselves
and are pursuing uplifting ways
of treating themselves.

I am joyful.
I am compassionate.
I am creative.
I am helpful.
I am.

DEALING WITH YOURSELF

Today is a day to reminisce,
today is a day to ponder.
Today is a day to scrutinize
your ways of dealing with yourself
and all people around you.

Are you honest?
Are you credible?
Are your best features displayed?

Inadequacy is not in dealing with people.
Inadequacy is in dealing with yourself.
Inadequacy is about not being honest,
not being honest about yourself.

Inadequacy is a word, not an action.
Action is not being honest,
not being honest with yourself.

Be lovingly dealing with yourself.
Become your own best honest friend.

FEAR vs. JOY

FEAR IS A WAY OF POSTPONING

Fear is not a way of living.
Fear is a way of postponing
what needs to be done.
Fear is not the way.

Release all doubts. Release all fears.
Release thoughts that are negative.
Be willing to indulge yourself
and live the life that is not at all frightful
but is an enjoyable way to live.

Fear is a quality of the mind
that inhibits it to the point
that your growth is unstable
and your growth is hindered.

It may be tolerable to some point,
however, if not changed
then it can lead to a great,
very great stagnation
of the body, mind, and spirit.

Listen to your fears not.
Do not be fearful ever again.
The Universe is with you all the way,
all is set to flourish.

The Universe is ready
to bequest you a rose,
a rose of knowledge,
that is growing, growing, growing.

27

PRECARIOUS LIVING

Precarious living is a malady.
It is an abandonment of fears for other fears.
Such as, I don't want to feel fearful,
therefore I will
jump off the bridge, ride a big fish,
will tell all I am pregnant when I am not.

This precarious living
is a sign of an inner instability
that is stemming from your inability
to comprehend
you are a person that is a Spirit
that lives in flesh,
and therefore does not comprehend
her true reality.

Not knowing your true reality is a pretext
as you truly know who you are.
Your true reality is you,
a Spirit, coming to Earth,
coming to elevate
yours and others searching.

DON'T GRAVITATE TOWARD HEAVY

Your state of mind may be not too pretty.
Your state of mind may be not too robust.
Your state of mind may be so, so
when you are dealing with fears.

Your fears are about many things:
I am not used to this...
'maybe' is the word...
I am irresponsible...
I am authoritative...

Therefore, your thoughts
gravitate toward heavy-heavy
and then you cannot look dewy,
as heaviness results in lines,
and heaviness is not
a way to live.

It is not a way to conduct yourself.
It is not a way to elaborate
on a given scenario
that is in the making
and continuing to grow
toward heavy-heavy.

ALLEVIATE YOUR WORRIES

Worrying is not the way
of spending your day.
Worrying is a problematic way
of alleviating your worries.

Stop the game called frustration.
The sooner the better you leave it behind,
is not soon enough.

Train yourself to appoint yourself
to be your own sole caretaker.
Your caretaker, your friend.
That is the way
to stay in touch with yourself.

Be on top of your own craft
floating toward a point on your map,
a map of the medley of different events
linked together by you.
You are your own map charter
and you are your own maker
of your destiny.

Quiet down your mind.
Listen to your heart.
You can do as you please,
but if you cannot alleviate your worries
then the sooner the better
will not be coming.

BROODING IS A WAY TO MISERY

Melancholy is an object
that rears its head
when you do not object
to being stricken by fear.
Fear is melancholy's dear,
very dear friend.

Other friends are worry and doubt.
Worry, fear, and doubt
have might over you
when you allow them to get to you.

When you can spot them
as far as they are
and then don't allow them
to come near you
then you cannot brood
and melancholically sit around.

See the circle?
You invite fear and worry
then you brood in melancholy
to create a cacophony
of further fears and worries.

Brooding is not what you want to do.
Brooding is not a way to pass your life.
Brooding is a way to self-made misery,
misery of fears and doubts.

ACTIVATE JOY TO BREED JOY

Be free with joy,
with gaiety, with happiness.
Do not forget to live, to smile,
to smell simple flowers.

Melancholy is out. Joy is in.
Melancholy is the theft of God's gift to you.
Life is precious. Life is joy.
Enjoy, enjoy,
enjoy God's gift of life.

Joy is a matter that can be felt
as it vibrates and churns
through space and the Universe,
through space forever and ever.

Joy is a substance
that can be attracted by others.
Then the joy multiplies
and radiates through all.

Do enjoy
the possibility of joy multiplying.
If you cannot exude joy
then you may destroy
the chance of joy filling the space.

Activate joy to breed joy.

YOU ARE A FREE BIRD

Do not be unclear about
who you are.
Do not be unclear about
how to figure out who you are.

Do not be milling about
in indecisions about your life.
Do not be a bird that is lost.
The answers are within.

How do I unearth them,
you may ask.

There are many,
who just like you
are asking, who are you
and who am I?

You are a Soul
that is listening to God's whispers,
that is listening to all
that is surrounding you,
that is beckoning you.

You are a free bird, a Soul,
flying through times of eternity.
You are a Soul that is.

MAKE YOUR LIFE FUN

Are you a person who is waiting?
Who is waiting and waiting
instead of taking action?
Who is waiting and waiting
and losing faith in interaction?

Who is not totally sure?
Who is not clear about the next step
that is to be taken
in the march through eternity?

Trust that all will become clear.
That all will be anew.
That all will be colour and the bright sun.
That all will be immortal fun.
That all will be, as you can imagine,
fun, fun, fun.

Make your life fun.
Make your life unending fun.
Make your life easy and all smiles.
Make your life something
that is not an unwelcome chore.
Make your life fun.

Boost your confidence by saying
I am confident a hundred times.
Boost your confidence by saying
I am confident and I trust.

Boost your confidence by saying
ooh la la, I am not fearing
anything and anybody.
I am ready to embark on a new journey.
I am a person of vision.

YOU ARE FIRST

YOU ARE WORTH EVERY PENNY

Say to yourself
that you are worth every penny,
that you are benevolently spending money,
as anything you desire is here for the taking—
your clothes, your yearnings,
your other possessions.

You are not in a regression
when you are on a spending spree.

However, the way you spend is important.
How do you spend?
Willingly, happily
or grudgingly with fear?

If you regret what you did
then spending is not the way to go.
If you enjoy your possessions
then you can start building toward letting go.

Let go and just be,
let go and willingly
decide to either spend or not.

To have or not to have
is not the question.
Simple having is not a sin.
To have a lot is not a sin.
To flaunt it and worship it is.

LISTEN TO YOUR OWN BEAT

Health and love are the substance of life.
How do you know you are healthy?
How do you know?
There is a way of telling, you know.

It is not when you sneeze
and you need to be put at ease.
And someone says,
oh, be with us, do not go yet,
we need you here to support us.
You, please you, get healthy, you,
we depend on you.

You are healthy if you sneeze
and do not mind if you cough,
as it does not mean a thing,
as you are healthy in your mind.
Those are just superficial little things
that are on the surface
and are not ingrained within.

You can obliterate them at your will,
when your mind is healthy
and you are not dwelling on the things
that are not wealthy.

Listen to the voice within.
Listen to your own beat.
Be within, in your own reach.
Keep in mind you are first
and then the rest is easy.

Look after yourself.
Be kind to yourself.
Be attentive to yourself—
you are first.

FOLLOW THE PATH OF YOUR DESIRE

Follow the path of your desire.
Dress yourself in the attire
of love, of understanding, of compassion
for yourself and your companions.

Life is a way of determining who you are,
of determining that you are
the most important one in the whole world.

You are the one who needs to be told
life is yours to take and behold.
You are your own maker and your own caretaker.
You are your own boss and pleasure maker.
You are your own.

What is good for you makes you good.
What is good for you
is to be engaging and giving to others,
to be joyful, calm, and mellow.

It will follow you everywhere you go.
It will give you a nice fresh glow
that will make you look
like every morning of every day
you bathe in a brook
of fresh scented waters.

DON'T OBEY YOUR EGO

Ego is on guard at all times.
It is searching and seeking
for what it will hurt and what will hurt it.
It is always ready to be hurt.

Are you that ego?
You are it, if you allow it to be.
And that you can do rather easily,
looking for hurts,
real or imaginary.

Don't be a victim of your ego.
Know who wants what.
Is it you, the real you,
or is it your impostor, your ego?

Separate the chaff from the grain.
If you allow your ego to go
it is how you will glow,
glow and gleam, and be happy.

JUST BE

BEING

Nature is not a mindless body.
Nature has a consciousness.
Nature is a beautiful example of just being,
as nature is not at all thinking
ah, my, my, what shall I do next,
but is creating with intent
and is surging, full of life.

Be like nature.
Nature is a perfect solution.
It is not brimming with resolutions,
with thoughts, with quotes and arguments.
Nature is, and that is enough.
Nature is, and that is its purpose.

Just as nature,
your purpose is in being and not doing.
Your purpose is in existence
and not in proving that you are the best,
that you are on a quest,
that you are linked with someone
who is prolific and successful.

Being,
a quiet, slow rendering of your thoughts,
of your needs, of your elementary pleasures,
of your basic nature
that is you.

BE LIKE NATURE, JUST BE

Nature is a pleasant stroll through the meadows.
It is a pleasant awakening to the songs of birds.
It is a nullifying effect of winds.
It is stormy waters coming down from clouds.

Nature is a respectful and loving mother.
But she can also be angry like no other.
Nature is of a similar aspect to God—
it is immense, and it is not.

Nature creates its own.
It creates an everlasting bounty
of shapes, colours, sounds, sights.
Above all, it is, is, is.

Nature is.
Be like nature. Be.
Create, enjoy, exist.

Nature and you have a common source.
Nature and you are living entities.
Nature and you are. You both exist.

NATURE IS THE WAY TO BE

You and nature were created by God.
He is residing in you,
He is calling from within you.
He is trying to get from within without
so you can experience Him a lot,
every second of your life.

Beast within you is a beast of hope
and nature has no hope,
for she does not need it.
Nature is always at its best.
It is not hoping for a rerun,
saying, if this and that would not have happened
I would be happier today.

Be like nature.
Exist.
Be like nature and do not pretend
that your happiness depends on others' opinion,
that your happiness is based on where you fit.

It is not.
You can exist
without being classified as important,
as someone who is absent or impatient,
as someone who is not like nature.

Nature.
That is the way to be.

LEARN FROM NATURE

Nature is calm.
Nature is ready to strike.
Nature is omnipotent,
she is gentle and wise.

If she needs it,
nature has a potency to claim her own
and if not, then she will spit out that
which she does not want.

How does nature decide
what should be spat out?

Well, it is easy.
She is not deciding for you or others;
she is deciding for herself.

See the parallel?
If you decide for yourself,
and then take charge of your own,
the world will be governed by those
who should take charge
and not by those
who should not.

Best of all is to believe in you.
Best of all is to approve of you.
Approval of yourself is the way to live.
Approval of yourself is the way to believe
that you, only you, can guide you.

Be like nature.
Claim your own
and spit out that which is unneeded.

SMELL THE ROSES ALL THE TIME

Unwell thoughts out,
nice thoughts in.
Negative thoughts out,
positive thoughts in.
What does it mean?

You are given powers,
right now at this moment,
to dissolve all your thoughts
that are running and mulling around.

It is your own mind,
so use it and stop the rush!
Next, put in happy thoughts.

Be like a breeze of fresh air,
a breeze of new ideas and thoughts
that are positively inwardly rooted,
with the intent to look after yourself.

Applaud others for their successes.
Spell your name correctly
for angels to recognize you.
Spill no beans,
and smell the roses all the time.

BE YOUR OWN

Take your share of the joy,
your share of the pleasure,
your share of a laugh,
and treasure, oh, so treasure
your freedom,
your freedom to use your will.

Use your will. Use your intuition.
Use your apparent charm.
Use your decisive thinking.
Use your meditative nature.

Be what you are.
Be within and without.
Be wise and large.
Be, be, be.

Be like a bee,
which flutters from flower to flower
drinking the nectar
and processing its power
into a honey that serves all
with a nourishing sweet nectar
of life and love.

Be at peace.
Be readily at peace.
Be your own teacher and preacher.
Be your own unending corrector.
Be your own everlasting protector.

Be your own minimally limited enthusiast.
Be your own blatantly happy person.
Be your own rightfully crazy analyst.
Be your own.
That is all you need,
be your own.

Your own lover, friend, teacher,
preacher, host, and guest,
as you are on a quest
of discovering your blueprint.

LOVE

SMELL THE ROSES OF GODLY LOVE

Love. Love that is not lost
and lustfully overpowered by the senses,
that has not lost its true meaning,
that is so warm and beaming
that you quiver from pleasure
which is not of fleshly origin,
that is an everlasting cosmic vibration,
that is love pouring from every cell,
that is love, as God intended it to be,
the spiritual inferno of love
that swallows all other loves,
that encompasses your ever-hungry ego.

Ego. Ego that is not you,
that thrives on the meaningless,
that sabotages your seeking,
that is on guard and is always speaking
when it feels not to be honoured,
that is superficially entrenched
in the physical reality,
that is your enemy if you keep on listening,
that is your own doom.

Wake up and smell the roses of godly love.
Be prepared not to dwell only into material realms.
Be prepared to accumulate wealth
that cannot be translated into money,
that is not measurable in gold,
that is not perceivable through market fallacy
of demand and supply.

REPLACE THE MILITARY WITH LOVE

Military is an upbringing of humanity.
Military is a way of living.
Compete. Fight.
Military, all military might.
Military is a way of life on Earth,
enemies and wars.
Military is a way of life.

Why do we talk about military?
Why do we think of military?
Well, this decade is not going to change,
this decade you will be aware
of military happenings.

Military is not love, military is fright.
Military is a fear of others and yourself.
Military is a way of conceiving
that others are enemies.

Military is a way of thinking
that you are in danger.
Military is a way of saying,
if I strike first, then you must,
you must subjugate yourself to me.
Then I win. Then I will lead.
Then I will conquer.

To conquer others is not the way to go.
To conquer yourself is the way.
Conquer your fears.
Conquer your shortcomings,

such as military thoughts about others,
and replace them with love.

Love is a sheath that is healing,
that is protecting,
that reflects who you are—
a spiritual being.
Love is a way of being with God,
God that is within and is waiting
to be brought without.

Military is your past,
as you have always raised the mast
of military thoughts.
Down with the military; up with love.

Your mast must be the one
where all can feel safe,
where all can hope to come and be blessed.
To feel safe from a military way
of reproaching themselves,
of accommodating military thoughts.

Peace to all on this Earth.
Love to all on this planet,
this blue, blue, watery planet
that is a crib for all.

BESTOW YOUR LOVE ON ALL

Desdemona is a literary figure, or is she?
She is a devotee of love, who is slain,
who is not awarded plain,
plain love back,
but is awarded jealousy.

Jealousy is a feeling
when your fixation overpowers your senses
and dictates nonsenses,
such as she loves me
but she also loves others.

Love can be misunderstood.
Love can be a fleeting thing.
It can be used as a possessive power
over other beings.

Love, as a healing agent, is missing
in many people's lives,
as they are not allowing themselves
to be at ease in their love with loves.

To truly love large is what we need to achieve,
as love is a beautiful feeling
and is here to be shared with every being.

Bestow your love on others without strings.
Bestow your love without oppressing them.
Bestow your love in a quiet way.
Bestow your love as gently as you can.

Bestow your love in a loving way,
not in a way of a tyrant,
who presumes that love gives him a right
to control any object he loves.

Love is a mesmerizing feeling
of being loved and loving others.
Love is a feeling of exuberance.
Love is a thought of happiness.
Love is a way to be.

YOUR LOVE BREEDS LOVE

Love yourself before others.
Express gratitude toward yourself
before you thank others.

Express love to yourself
in a tangible form:
I love you, for as I look at you,
you give me lots of joy.
I love you, as when you deal with me,
you are always gentle.

Why is this important? Why?
It is a principle of the Universe
that love is sustenance.
Love is food for your body and mind.

Hate is the opposite of love.
Hate is a feeling of being pushed into an existence
where your needs are not met.
It is a feeling of not being able to abandon yourself
to joy and exuberance.

Turn hate into love. Become free.
Clear the feeling
of living in an abyss of disillusionment,
of breaking your heart
every time someone says a thing
that is not what you think
they should be saying.

Those are your expectations.
Those are your rules.
If someone does not love you
as you think he should,
the remedy is to love yourself.

Bestow love on yourself.
Your love will reflect in all.
Your love will breed more love.
And you will see
that it will come back to you
from others and your Thee.

LOVE

Love is a feeling that is quite etheric.
Love is a feeling that is of the higher Spirit.
Love is a feeling of being one with others.

Love is a compassionate understanding
of your fellow human beings' needs,
of your fellow human beings' aspirations,
of your fellow human beings' advances,
reaching toward the stars,
reaching beyond present mass,
reaching beyond present times.

Love, falling in love, falling,
being in love, feeling,
feeling of being happy and joyous,
of creating a new life.

EARTHLY LOVE

Love is a noble, very noble feeling,
that leaves you many times reeling
in a sea of unhappiness. But why?

It is an earthly love for your human fellow.
It is love that is from delicate material,
as it can happen, oh, so suddenly,
that you lose your granted freedom
as you emotionally connect yourself to someone
and then you unravel that ball of thread
that you have come to dread
and sometimes even hate.

Why does earthly love turn to hate?
Why is it, why?

Love, as it is called on Earth,
is sometimes just an infatuation.
Infatuation with the male and female,
as different energy will prevail
and will attract one to another.

Love on Earth can cause you to lean
to one side too heavily.
Heavily, as in heavy with tears and emotions,
as in 'oh, I love you, only you' devotion.

It is a love that occupies itself with itself.
It is a love that is concerned with another human.
It is a love that is limited,
even if it can be so exuberant.

It is love, as you know it,
as you wrote about it
in your love sonnets and other poetry,
in another lifetime.

HEAVENLY LOVE

What is heavenly love?
It is love that is deep,
that is so deep and warm,
that it does not take you by storm
but evolves as you mature into it.

It is love that is so beautiful,
love that is so plentiful.
It is a kind of love
that will withstand all time
anything.

This type of love is immensely uplifting.
It negates anything that happened before.
It engulfs all that went on
for eons of time,
from the beginning to the end.

Oh, that love, that love is so powerful
that it will give you plentiful
energy and joy,
manliness, womanhood,
great thoughts and absolute power
over any tainted ploy.

It is a love of recognition that all is one.
This love is a most beautiful song.
It is a most beautiful way of feeling alive,
of feeling a part
of the Universe.

We cannot make you understand
this feeling of love.
This feeling of love can be had
only through experiencing that
exuberant wonderful love
that is your universal truth
that will open the gate to flood you
with knowledge and understanding.

LOVE AS AN EMOTION OF YOUR LIFE

Stop, listen,
do as your heart is telling you.

You want to be, so be.
You want to play, so play.
What is so hard about that?
Just do it! Just follow your heart.

Yesterday, you were laughing
and you were also sad.
You were happy and you were glad,
also unhappy and then mad.

Emotions are not what you should listen to.
Emotions are a way of seeing
this way or the other way,
any way that is coloured by emotions.

Assure that priorities are straightened out,
that love is an emotion of your life,
that all your acts are pure
and clearly defined from your heart.

Assure that love is an emotion of your life.

LOVE IS NOT BASED ON DUTIES

Less is more when demanding submission.
Less is more when demanding accord.
Submission is not what you want.
Submission is not what makes you grow.

Submit yourself to others' wishes
and your Soul is neglected.
Submit yourself to others
and they become a pain,
someone you always worry and think about.

Does he or does he not?
Does he want me to do it or not?

True love is not based on demands and duties.
True love is not based on responsibilities.
You are responsible only to yourself,
for your conduct
that should be of the best,
of the best, clearest and purest intent.

Love is a mutual understanding that you are one
and a member of the whole.
Love is a feeling
that you are not alone,
that you belong to whales,
dolphins, tigers, rocks,
that you can do anything at its max,
as you are a child of the Universe.

Do not submit to others' wants.
Listen to your heart.
If it says no, do not.
If it says yes, then go full speed ahead.

THROUGH LOVE

Project love at all times.
Love is essential
for human beings to soar en masse
to another reality
where the vibrations are higher,
where the vibrations were acquired
through loving all kind.

Know that virtue is to be self-realized.
Know that being self-realized
comes from a position of trust
that you, as a God being,
you, God,
have the power of making the Earth heaven
for the whole of mankind,
through love.

PROJECT LOVE AT ALL TIMES

Project love at all times.
Be the object of your love.
When you love yourself
you are not inclined to judge.
You are at peace with yourself
and you can see and understand
those who are not living their life right.

Do you tell them that you believe
they are not living right?
Is that what you ought to do?
If they ask, if they need your support,
please do.
Otherwise, it is up to them
to understand their responsibilities,
to realize they need to deal
with the life they lead.

Love unconditionally.
In unconditional love
is your power of deriving your happiness,
of deriving your infallible feeling of giddiness,
of being giddy with your truthful and loving ways
of embracing yourself
and others.

LOVE IS KNOWING

Love is an exhilarating feeling of knowing
that you and your love
are on the same wavelength,
that you and your love are duly taking off
and are heading toward
the promised land.

Land, that land, you came from.
That land which is joyous and wonderful.
That land that is waiting for you.
The land that You, God,
promised you.

LOVE IS A MELTING POT

Love is an everlasting joy,
if you understand that love,
true love, does not mean an infatuation
with that which is on the surface,
with that which is fleeting.

Love is compassion and understanding.
Love is a feeling of joy, of openness,
of unending rapture,
of loving every part of nature
that encompasses the entire picture,
from a rock to a human being.

Situations, in their simplicity or complexity,
situations, looked at with love,
are always simple to resolve.
All, virtually, absolutely, all,
is melted within the pot of love.

Love is a melting pot, a unifying force
that you do not understand that well,
in this physical dimension so steeped
in a very deep, non-spiritual realm.

Love is omnipresent, it is cleansing.
It rinses you of dark and mundane thoughts.
It is an evolutionary step
toward enlightening your race,
inevitable through your journey
back to your origins.

SUBSTANCE OF THE UNIVERSE

Death is an equalizer. It equalizes all
and nobody can break away from it at all.
Death is the entry to life
that is not understood by you,
as it is not a way you deal with life on Earth.

Life on Earth can be a way of atoning,
particularly if you do not understand
that you are a Soul,
a breathing, living individual,
a living Soul on your planet Earth.
That you are not bones and flesh
but are composed of ethereal matter
that is not dense, that is a known substance
of the whole Universe, that is love.

Love is a substance that is you.
Love is a feeling of exuberance
when you can tell that all is well.
Love is when you want to resolve the issues
and you do not leave them to swell.

Love is all encompassing.
Love is a power that propels all.
Love is a feeling of fulfillment.
Love is a song that is rising high.
Love is a virtue that God gave us.

Love is a feeling among all
that was created by him
who we call God.

LOVE IS LIFE

Galaxies are not what you see.
Galaxies are Soul sights.
Galaxies are free of melancholy.
Galaxies are love.

Love is your prime concern.
Love is not separate from life.
Love is life.

Love is a way of plunging yourself into living.
Love is a material, also esoterical, way of feeling
the pulse of life in you, in others.
Do not avoid love.
Love is life.

Love is life. Love is the way.
Love is a precious balance
between knowing and feeling.
Love is the way.

Love is a feeling of sadness rolled into happiness.
Love is a feeling of mundane rolled into lofty.
Love is a feeling of a mesmerizing,
never-ending, rolling, bouncing flow of energy,
flowing unceasingly and unguardedly,
with no limitations.

Love.
Love is a must.
Without love all dies.
Without love all is arid.

Without love all annihilates itself.
Without love there is no hope.
Without love there is no shine.
Without love there is no amour.

Love.

GOD'S LOVE IS AN ENDLESS RAPTURE

Love is a feeling of exuberance
within your body and your mind.
Love is a feeling of belonging.
Love is a perfect solution to living.
Love is a mesmerizing, mesmerizing feeling.
Love is.

Love is a feeling
of you belonging to the Universe.
Love takes you away
from your atoll of self-pity,
of self-disparaging comments,
of self-deprecating thoughts,
of loneliness, of separation,
of those feelings and acts
that impact your physical reality.

Love raises your vibration.
It raises your feeling of belonging.
It raises your expectations of yourself
to feel, to be, to act
as one with God.

Love is that all encompassing feeling
that you are reeling, reeling in happiness,
in wonderful, giddy happiness.
Oh, how true it is, how true,
but if you actually knew
that love can be even bigger.

Love, as in God's love, is an incredible power.
It is an endless rapture.
Why don't you learn how to capture
that everlasting joy of God?

YOUR HEART IS THE SEAT OF THE SPIRIT

True love is a quality
that is rare among you.
As perceived and practiced on Earth,
love can be an infatuation affair.

True love is a warm feeling.
True love can move mountains.
It can traverse continents.
It can help you to understand.

To join with another is to honour oneself.
To join in love is an honour bestowed on you.
To join in love is the perpetual motion
of energy flowing into material.

Joining your bodies is an act of love
that is expressed in flesh.
Joining in heart is love
that is expressed in Spirit,
as your heart is the seat of the Spirit,
a gate to your oneness in all.

HEART

YOUR HEART IS NOT ONLY A PUMP

The heart is an organ.
The heart is important,
so very important.
The heart is a leading expert
on matters of love.

The heart is the determining factor
of your evolution,
of your approach to life.
The heart is an organ
that pumps your blood.

The heart is pumping blood,
is swelling with pride
and is shrinking inside
if you are not living from love.

Love is the truth and the heart knows it.
The heart is an open path
throughout your evolution to meet your God.
The heart is a path that leads to God.

The heart is spreading thinly
if you cannot see even dimly
that your etheric heart[1],
the counterpart
to your physical heart,
can elevate you within
toward your maker, your God.

---

[1] The etheric heart is believed to be the Seat of the Soul.

85

The heart is an open gateway to other worlds.
It is a gateway.
Your heart is a priceless way
of contacting your maker, your God.

KEEP YOUR HEART CLEAR

If you keep your heart clean and clear,
if your heart is vivid, alive and caring,
if your heart is ready to take action
when your heart sees an aberration,
when others need help,
when others yelp
and your heart is ready to come
and extend its goodness, its advice,
then you will entice
the way that will take you home,
home to your maker, God.

There is a way
to contact your God
through your heart.
The heart is a powerful organ.
It is a gateway.

Keep it clean and open.
Keep it listening
for the cries of other people
who might benefit from your help,
and you will benefit as well.

WITH ALL MY HEART

I am yourself, your very own Self,
that is sometimes called your Higher Self.
Rest assured you and I are one.

Pleasing, as it may feel, I am at your will.
It is easy to do, as I am not your enemy.
How could I be your enemy,
if I am you and you are me?

I love you with my all heart.
I love you,
as I am you and you are me.

You are well endowed with a heart,
and that means to me
you are capable of loving the me
that is you,
with a full and open heart.

I LOVE YOU

I love you with a full and open heart,
a heart that does not quit
when it's difficult to understand
that the heart is an organ to bequest love
and hold it close.

Close, oh, so close,
so it does not get scared.
Close, oh, so close,
so it does not veer away.
Close, so close, as close
as it can be.

Closeness is a quality to behold.
Closeness is the quality
that will make humankind forget
that it had any malady.

Closeness is a very warm feeling.
It is a quality
that makes the world forget inequality.

The heart is your everlasting joy.
The heart is your everlasting,
ever encompassing joy
of giving yourself to all.

IN YOUR HEART YOU KNOW IT ALL

Little Jesus, who was a real boy,
a Saint of the previous era,
came to Earth to show to all
that bliss is real if you not only kneel
but mainly do as follows:
speak the truth,
be brave and honest,
be true,
true to your heart.

Your heart is your leader.
Your heart is your guide.
Your heart is that which is taught
by Spirit.

Spirit talks to your heart,
and your heart follows Spirit.
Your heart then presses
against your consciousness
that is steeped in its own righteousness
of being an earthly being.

If the heart is your guide
then you understand and start
on the path of enlightenment.

Your heart grows and grows
until it becomes engrossed
with love for all humanity.

Then, in this state of enlightenment,
future evolution happens
until you meet your Creator
who reveals to you all
that you needed to know.

YOU KNOW THAT YOU KNOW

You will find out your origins,
you will find out your source,
you will find out your purpose,
your purpose in life,
life that can be mundane or great.

The scale does not really make
the importance of the purpose.
Important is all,
does not matter if big or small.

Important is to reveal
your origins and your source.
Please do not think
that you are on the brink
of a big, big discovery,
as in your heart you know it all.

You know who you are.
You know what you are,
and you know that you know.

SEXUALITY

SEX IS PURE IF YOU ARE PURE

Be like a pure flower
that is not wilting when someone is tilting,
tilting toward you,
to take a whiff of its sweet scent.

Be like a flower, pure, pure, pure.
Be of the purest, most beautiful scent.
Be one of the most beautiful scents
in the garden of God.

Be original, be sweet, be absolutely sure
that you see all as pure. That you see all
with childlike innocence from your heart,
with trust, unspoiled by ego and pride.

Be of pure innocence
of the thought and the act.
Perceive all as pure,
all that you encounter and do
in this world, on this Earth.

Sex is a part of humanity
and can be a perpetual item of wondering.
Should we or not? Is it clean?

Being pure is a state of being.
Sex is pure when the mind is pure.
Sex is a means of approving of life
in celebration of life with your love,
with your love partner,
with your life partners.

SEX IS NOT KEEPING YOU DOWN

Through your partner, you are teaching you,
using the relationship as a sounding board,
using the ties of love to find out who you are,
to find out that you can be the one
that is pure, whatever you do.

If your thoughts are pure, you are pure.
Sex is clean when the mind is clean.
Sex is not meant to proliferate
bondage and hatred.

Sex is a venting of your earthly needs.
Sex is a pacifier... or is it?
It is not, if you do not believe it.
It is up to you to believe what you need.
It is up to you to encounter your own beast.

We are not here to advise you on sex matters.
We are here to teach you
that you are not an earthling,
that your origins are of an unearthly type,
that you are a child of the stars.
Your sex is not our concern.
Your sex is something that you need to discern.

Do I need it or not?
Do I owe it to myself or what?
Do I find pleasure here on Earth?
Do I count the days and be blessed?

Do I encounter my own sexuality
and pass it over?
Do I succumb to the earthly urges
until all is over and then
I will be a star being
that is pure and white?

Sex is not keeping you down.
Sex is pure if you are pure.
Pleasure is a healthy thing in life.
Pleasure is a stuff of life.

Sex is fine if that is what you are,
and it is not, if that is not your area.
It is all up to you.
To whom do you listen, yourself or others?

That is the question you need to answer
for yourself.
Who are your bosses?
Others or your consciousness?

SEXUALITY IS GOD'S GIFT

What is keeping you from knowing?
Is it you, your made up reality?
Is it your preschool understanding
that is interfering with sexuality?

Sexuality that lies dormant,
sexuality that is benign,
sexuality that is so potent
that it cannot be described.

Sexuality that is human and spiritual,
that is simple and also a ritual,
sexuality that is not about sex.

Sexuality that is God's gift,
that is a revelation of a knowledge
seeded into your bodies
by the Creator who is seeded in you.

Sexuality is the thing that is not fully known,
as part of it is not of this world.
Part of it is a Spirit rising
from the loins of a human form.

A human form that is not of this world,
that was created in the worlds beyond,
beyond this Earth and beyond this reality.
A human form that is an expression
of the Spirit in your world.

DREAMLAND

CONTEMPLATE ON YOUR DREAMS

Direct contact with God happens at night,
therefore sleep is very beneficial.
If you do not sleep enough,
you are losing input that is valuable.

It is a life that is especially valuable.
It is life on a raw level,
on a raw, core level of your being.

Your dreams are a way of talking to God.
Your dreams are very real,
are of a more real substance
than your life on Earth.

Contemplate on your dreams.
They will become clear.
They will give you clear sight to decide
where to go, where to direct your steps,
where to clean and where to dust,
where to relieve your lust.

They will let you know
if your demands are growing too much
in a direction
that is not a direction to go.

IN SLEEP YOU CONTACT GOD

Life in a body is one conscious stream,
one conscious stream of awakening
and going to sleep.

Sleep is a need, a bodily need,
a spiritual need.
In sleep, you contact God—yourself.
God, as yourself, needs contact from you
and is waiting to be spoken to.

If you do, she always replies,
she always musters strength in you
to carry on
your divine blueprint plan.

Your blueprint plan of living
a life of beauty and harmony,
of material disposition
to the point of coalition with your Soul,
and leaving the body altogether.

BUT WHAT IS A DREAM?

What is it that makes you say pleasant dreams?
What is it that is always there,
that other people care
to tell you, have pleasant dreams?

Grace is bestowed upon you
when you sleep.
You are in dreamland purposely,
and your dreams are a way of finding
your focus in life.

Hence, the big hope
when looking into a dream dictionary.
Hence, the big dreams
when there is a positive sign.
Hence, a disappointment
when the dictionary will decline
the meaning you interpreted.

But what is a dream?
Is it worth thinking about?

A dream is a way of contact
between you and your Higher Self.
A dream is a part of yourself
that you don't know too well.

It is a piece of you that is close and near.
It is your Higher Self that is reaching you
in your dream.

DREAMS ARE IMPORTANT

Dreaming is pleasant
and sometimes worrisome.
Dreaming is sometimes quarrelsome,
as you quarrel with yourself,
your friends, and God.

Dreaming is a way to discover yourself.
Dreaming is a way to learn about yourself.
Dreaming is a way to find out the next step
that will provide you with an insight
into your current situation,
and will offer a period of a probation
in which you can change
the way you live.

Dreams are an important tool
to find your quest,
to deal with your past, future and present.
They represent you, as you are and want to be.
You, as you are, when at night you dream
and talk to yourself as your Higher Self.

Dreams are the way to direct you.
They are the way to coach you
to the point of understanding
that yes, oh yes, I am here
to discover that, oh dear, my dear,
I am God and I'd better behave as such.

ABOUT THE AUTHOR

Helena Kalivoda is an award-winning author devoted to sharing inspirational messages that support readers in transforming their lives. Lives of peace and happiness can be available to those who learn the power of creation through an open heart as encouraged by Helena's books.

AWAKEN! Spirit Is Calling, Helena's first book, contains powerful truths for each person's journey. These poignant teachings were downloaded from Helena's guides and angels. Be prepared for your 'aha' moments when reading the book.

Her second book, *WAKE UP! Your Heart Is Calling*, leads readers to realize that all aspects of humanity, when denied pure love, are bound to eventually fail and cannot be healthy. This book connects to an online environment where you can access extended resources to help you apply the learned principles.

WAKE UP! Prosperity Is Calling, Helena's third book, outlines The Seven Principles to Living a Life of Prosperity. These principles will become your truth and experience once you use them and live them consistently.

Currently, Helena is working on a new series of *Purposeful Mind* books of poetry. This book, *Contemplation*, is the third book of the series.

Helena holds a BA in Economics and B.Sc. in Computer Science. She is a mother of three, living in Canada. In 1997, she left the corporate world to continue the writing she started in the early nineties.

Visit www.booksbyhelena.ca for more information about Helena Kalivoda's books.

www.ingramcontent.com/pod-product-compliance
Lightning Source LLC
LaVergne TN
LVHW091202080426
835509LV00006B/793